SMART ABOUT

History

THE WRIGHT BROTHERS TAKE OFF

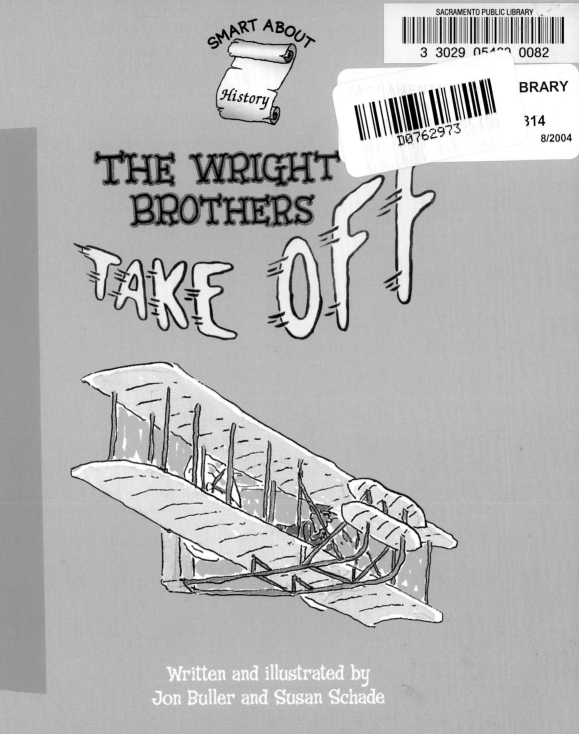

Written and illustrated by
Jon Buller and Susan Schade

Grosset & Dunlap → New York

For the Hawthornes—

Be good!

Do well!

Have fun!

Visit Jon Buller and Susan Schade at their web site www.bullersooz.com!

P. 4, 18, 23, Courtesy of Special Collections and Archives, Wright State University; p. 11, 25, Bettmann/Corbis; p. 24, Smithsonian Institution Photographic Service, National Museum of Air and Space; p. 27, Library of Congress.

Copyright © 2003 by Jon Buller and Susan Schade. All rights reserved. Published by Grosset & Dunlap, a division of Penguin Young Readers Group, 345 Hudson Street, New York, NY 10014. GROSSET & DUNLAP is a trademark of Penguin Group (USA) Inc. Published simultaneously in Canada. Manufactured in China.

Library of Congress Cataloging-in-Publication Data is available.

ISBN 0-448-42899-7   (pb)   A B C D E F G H I J

ISBN 0-448-43240-4   (GB)   A B C D E F G H I J

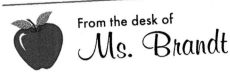

From the desk of

Ms. Brandt

Dear Class,
   We have been learning about so many exciting events from the past. Now you may choose a subject that is of special interest to you for your report.
   You may write about something that happened thousands of years ago or about something that happened not so very long ago – maybe when your parents or your grandparents were your age. It's up to you!

   Here are some questions you might want to think about:

What made you pick your topic?

Did you learn anything that really surprised you?

Good luck and have fun!
                                             Ms. Brandt

THE WRIGHT BROTHERS

I'M WILBUR. I'M THE OLDER ONE.

I'M ORVILLE. I'M THE ONE WITH THE MUSTACHE.

Wilbur Wright and Orville Wright were brothers. They were just ordinary guys who liked to make stuff, like kites and bicycles. But, in 1903, they did something that nobody had ever done before—they made an airplane that people could really fly in! How cool is that?! Their <u>Flyer I</u> looked like this

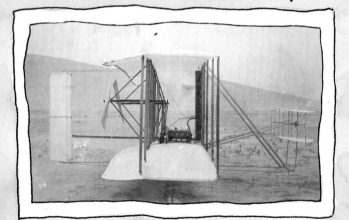

IT WAS MADE OF WOOD AND CLOTH. IT WAS 8 FEET HIGH, WITH A WINGSPAN OF 40 FEET. IT WEIGHED 750 POUNDS.

I picked the Wright Brothers for my report because making model planes is my hobby. So far, I have made twelve model planes. (Some of them aren't very good.)

So where did the word AIRPLANE come from? A "plane" is a flat surface. Early flying contraptions with flat (or almost flat) wings were called "air-plane machines." Later, people shortened that to just "airplane."

I HAVE BEEN ON THREE AIRPLANE TRIPS.

People have wanted to fly probably ever since they saw birds in the sky. Before Orville and Wilbur, lots of people had tried to fly, on all kinds of weird stuff!

KITES

HEY! NO FAIR!

YOW!

IN BATTLES, KITES WERE SOMETIMES USED TO LIFT PEOPLE OVER WALLS.

The first kind of aircraft was the KITE. Kites are attached to the ground by a rope, or line. Nobody knows for sure when or where the first kite was invented, but it was probably more than two thousand years ago in the Far East.

FLAPPERS

Some people thought they could fly by wearing wings and flapping them like birds. (You can't!)

IF LEONARDO'S DESIGN HAD BEEN BUILT, IT MIGHT HAVE LOOKED LIKE THIS.

The famous artist Leonardo da Vinci lived from 1452 to 1519. He had lots of ideas about how to fly. And he drew plans for a flying machine. It looked good on paper, but it wouldn't have worked.

The Marquis de Bacqueville tried to flap himself over a river in Paris in 1742. He didn't make it. He's lucky he only broke his leg.

HOT-AIR BALLOONS

BUILT BY MONTGOLFIER BROTHERS IN FRANCE

In 1783, people took off in a hot-air balloon for the first time. I would love to do that some day.

FIRE UNDER THE BALLOON FILLED IT WITH HOT AIR

WHEN THE BALLOON WAS FULL OF HOT AIR, PEOPLE LET GO OF THE ROPES HOLDING IT DOWN.

These balloons float because they are lighter than air. How can that be? It's because hot air is lighter than cool air. When the air inside a balloon is heated, it makes the balloon float up. Lighter things rise up. You can see this when you blow bubbles into a glass of juice through a straw. The bubbles rise. That's because they're lighter than the juice.

BUBBLES RISE

GLIDERS

HANG GLIDER (1970S)

GLIDERS are heavier than air. But they can fly for a while if they start on high ground and coast down to a lower spot. In 1853, a man named Sir George Cayley built a glider and made someone test it—his coachman. It worked! But the coachman quit right after it landed. I don't blame him!

WAY TO GO!

THAT'S IT! I'M GETTING ANOTHER JOB!

GLIDER LIFTED OFF FROM A WAGON AS IT ROLLED DOWNHILL.

EARLY CONTRAPTIONS

This invention had round wings that pumped up and down like an umbrella. It didn't fly by itself, so Degen had to add a hot-air balloon.

1806 DESIGN BY JACOB DEGEN

1890 DESIGN BY M. A. DELPRAT

This flying bicycle was never actually built.

This 1890 plane had a small steam engine and flew for 164 feet, but there was no way to control it!

NO CONTROL IS MORE FUN!

1890 DESIGN BY CLEMENT ADER

THE "RIGHT" BROTHERS

So the Wright Brothers weren't actually the first to fly. But they are famous because their flying machine got everything right. (Well, almost everything.)

✓ Their plane was heavier than air. (In other words, not just a balloon.)
✓ It didn't have to land on lower ground. (Not just a glider.)
✓ It had an engine. (Made its own power.)
✓ And it could be controlled by a pilot. (Important!)

THIS 1908 FLYER WAS AN IMPROVED VERSION OF FLYER I. THE PILOT COULD SIT UP, INSTEAD OF LYING FLAT ON THE WING.

WHEN WILBUR AND ORVILLE WERE KIDS

Wilbur was born on April 16, 1867. Orville was born on August 19, 1871.

They lived most of their lives in the same house in Dayton, Ohio. Wilbur died there, and Orville was 43 years old when he finally moved out. All of the Wright kids had unusual family nicknames, except Lorin.

REUCHLIN "ROOSH"

LORIN

KATHARINE "SCHWESTERCHEN"

ORVILLE "BUBO"

WILBUR "ULAM"

THE WRIGHT KIDS
7 HAWTHORNE ST.
DAYTON, OHIO

PROPELLER →

RUBBER BAND MOTOR

PAPER

BAMBOO

Even when they were boys, Wilbur and Orville were interested in things that flew. In 1878, their father brought them a toy —a Chinese flying top. It was made out of cork and bamboo and paper, and used a twisted-up rubber band to send it flying.

UH-OH!

Wilbur and Orville played with their toy until it broke. Then they made more on their own. They called them "bats."

RUBBER-BAND POWER

I know about rubber-band power. Most of my model planes are powered by rubber. The rubber band attaches to wires on the propeller and in the tail. You wind the rubber band up by twirling the propeller around and around with your finger. When it is twisted up tight you let it go. It unwinds really fast and makes the propeller turn, just like an engine does.

You can learn a lot from toys and models. The Wright Brothers did from making "bats." And I have learned a lot about airplanes by making models. Did you know that some of the early air-flight inventors built small models to try out their ideas? That way, they didn't have to spend a lot of money to make full-sized flying machines, and also they couldn't get hurt trying to fly them!

Orville got his first bicycle in the early 1880s. He borrowed three dollars from Wilbur to buy it. In the early 1890s he bought a new "safety" bicycle for 160 dollars.

OLD KIND OF BICYCLE

A NEW KIND OF BIKE WAS DEVELOPED AROUND 1890. IT WAS CALLED A "SAFETY BICYCLE" BECAUSE THERE WASN'T SO FAR TO FALL.

Everybody wanted to ride these new bikes. And in 1892, Orville and Wilbur opened a bike shop—selling, renting, repairing, and building bicycles. You can see the Wright Brothers' actual shop in the Henry Ford Museum. It's in Dearborn, Michigan. I hope I can go there someday.

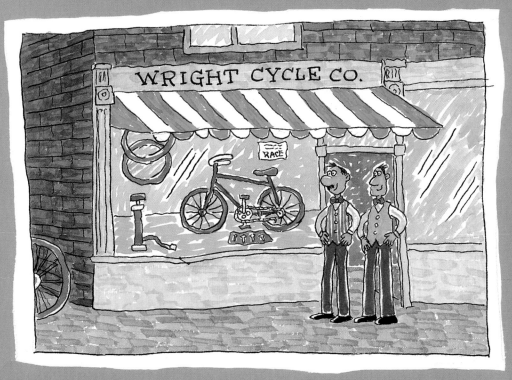

Their bike business was so successful that Wilbur and Orville had time to look around for something new and exciting to do.

IT WAS...

FLYING

THE WRIGHT BROTHERS LEARNED A LOT FROM THE GLIDERS OF A GUY NAMED OTTO LILIENTHAL.

The Wright Brothers decided they wanted to fly. They went to the library and read lots of books. (Like I did for this report!) They also wrote letters to people asking for information. (Too bad they didn't have the Internet back then.) The two of them thought a lot about how machines work.

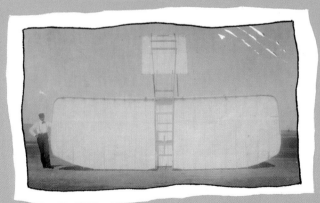

THE WRIGHT BROTHERS TOOK PHOTOGRAPHS TO MAKE RECORDS OF THEIR EXPERIMENTS.

They built stuff to try out their ideas. And they were careful to keep good records of their work.

PAPER AIRPLANES

The Wright Brothers learned about flying by trying out different ideas. Here is an experiment you can do yourself! Make a paper airplane, like this.

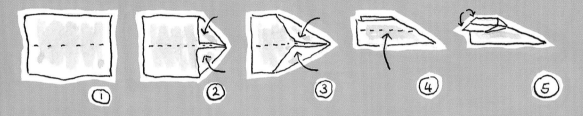

① ② ③ ④ ⑤

Now throw it. See?
It works like a glider.

GOOD SHAPE

It glides through the air
before it falls to the ground.

Now see what happens when you just crumple a piece of paper and try to fly it. It will fall right to the ground. That shows that the shape of a flying machine is important!

BAD SHAPE

KITTY HAWK

At last, Wilbur and Orville were ready to try and fly. They needed a place that had the right kind of weather for flying—strong winds and no trees. They picked Kitty Hawk, North Carolina. It was a small fishing village. There weren't very many houses, and there was a lot of wind and sand.

KITTY HAWK

700 MILES

DAYTON, OHIO

KITTY HAWK, NORTH CAROLINA

OUTER BANKS

On Thursday, September 6, Wilbur got on the in Dayton, Ohio. Twenty-four hours later, he got off at Old Point Comfort, Virginia. Then he took a across to Norfolk, Virginia. He spent the night in a hotel. On Saturday, he took a to Elizabeth City, North Carolina. Now he had only thirty miles to go, but it was across some water, and there wasn't a . It took Wilbur three more days just to find somebody to take him to Kitty Hawk. On Tuesday, he finally got a ride in a leaky . Then he sailed on a . But there was bad weather, and Wilbur had to wait out the storm.

Wilbur didn't get to until Wednesday night at 9:00. It had taken him six whole days to travel from Dayton to Kitty Hawk. That's only about 700 miles!

The Wright Brothers could only stay in Kitty Hawk after summer was over when their bike business slowed down. They went in September 1900, and again in 1901 and 1902. They put up a tent, and built a glider. They made some trial flights.

They had a lot of problems.

THEIR GLIDER GOT BURIED BY BLOWING SAND

THEY GOT ATTACKED BY MOSQUITOES.

OUCH! WHAP!

AND THERE WAS BAD WEATHER.

But they learned a lot. By the time they left in 1902, they had learned how to control the glider. They were ready to add the engine.

It isn't easy being an inventor. Nobody made the kind of engine Wilbur and Orville needed, so they had to build their own.

They also discovered that nobody could tell them what kind of propeller to use. They had to figure it out by themselves.

When they went back to Kitty Hawk, the weather was terrible. Their motor broke and they had to fix it, and it was getting cold. Pretty soon it would be too wintry for flying. Finally, on December 14, 1903, they were ready to try power flight.

OUCH!

WILBUR! ARE YOU ALL RIGHT?

THEIR FIRST TRY WAS NOT A SUCCESS, AND THEIR PLANE WAS SLIGHTLY DAMAGED.

FIRST FLIGHT

On December 17, 1903, after they had repaired the damage to their flying machine, they tried again. Wilbur once wrote in a letter that a person "positively must not take dangerous risks," but now he and Orville were too excited to be careful. They took their machine, <u>Flyer I</u>, out in very strong winds. It was Orville's turn to fly. . . . And he did!

→ The flight lasted only twelve seconds.
The <u>Flyer</u> went only 120 feet.
But still, it was a first!

The Wright Brothers made three more flights that day. The last one was the longest—852 feet in 59 seconds. Then, when the machine was on the ground, a gust of wind rolled it over and over and broke it. The Wright Brothers went home to Dayton.

Form No. 168.

THE WESTERN UNION TELEGRAPH COMPANY.

INCORPORATED

23,000 OFFICES IN AMERICA.   CABLE SERVICE TO ALL THE WORLD.

This Company TRANSMITS and DELIVERS messages only on conditions limiting its liability, which have been assented to by the sender of the following message. Errors can be guarded against only by repeating a message back to the sending station for comparison, and the Company will not hold itself liable for errors or delays in transmission or delivery of Unrepeated Messages, beyond the amount of tolls paid thereon, nor in any case where the claim is not presented in writing within sixty days after the message is filed with the Company for transmission.
This is an UNREPEATED MESSAGE, and is delivered by request of the sender, under the conditions named above.

ROBERT C. CLOWRY, President and General Manager.

170

RECEIVED at

176 C KA CS 33 Paid.   Via Norfolk   Va

Kitty Hawk N C Dec 17

Bishop M Wright

                    7 Hawthorne St

Success four flights thursday morning all against twenty one mile wind started from level with engine power alone average speed through air thirty one miles longest 57 seconds inform Press home Christmas .

                                        Orevelle Wright   525P

Newspaper reporters weren't very interested in the Wright Brothers' story. Other people had claimed to fly before and then turned out to be faking. The reporters thought that the Wright Brothers might be faking, too.

In 1904 and 1905, the Wright Brothers built <u>Flyer II</u> and <u>Flyer III</u>. They practiced in a cow pasture. They learned to fly in circles. They flew twelve miles, then they flew 24 miles. Over the next few years, they put on air shows for thousands of people.

In 1909, they formed the Wright Company, which built airplanes. Now, the Wright Brothers were successful and famous, but do you know what I think? I think they had more fun testing their gliders and flying machines than they did being famous.

WRIGHT BROTHERS MONUMENT

There is a national monument to the Wright Brothers in Kitty Hawk, North Carolina. It's right on the sand dunes where they flew <u>Flyer I</u>.

On the monument it says:
In commemoration of the conquest of the air by the brothers Wilbur and Orville Wright. Conceived by genius. Achieved by dauntless resolution and unconquerable faith.*

* Translation by my mom:
In honor of the first flight by the Wright Brothers, who had a great idea, stuck with it, and always believed in themselves.

WHAT THE WRIGHT BROTHERS FIGURED OUT
(and what came later)

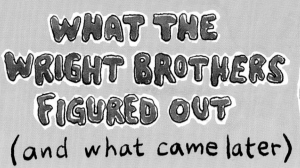

Earlier inventors thought an airplane's wings should flap like a bird's.

The Wright Brothers used wings that didn't move and propellers that did.

PROPELLER

But their propellers were in the rear. They pushed the plane.

Later on, propellers were put on the fronts of airplanes and pulled them. That generally worked better.

The Wright Brothers figured out that they could control tilting (when one wing goes higher than the other) by making wings that could be twisted.

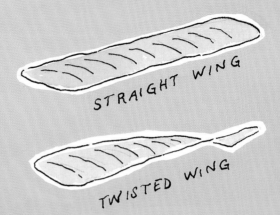

STRAIGHT WING

TWISTED WING

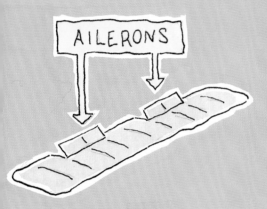

AILERONS

Later on, people found that it was better to control the tilt with adjustable flaps called "ailerons."

The Wright Brothers put the stabilizer (to control up and down movements) in the front. And the rudder (to control side to side movements) in the back.

Later, it was discovered that putting them both in the back worked better.

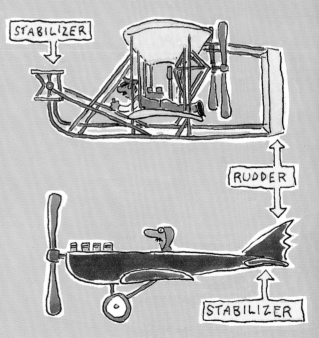

STABILIZER

RUDDER

STABILIZER

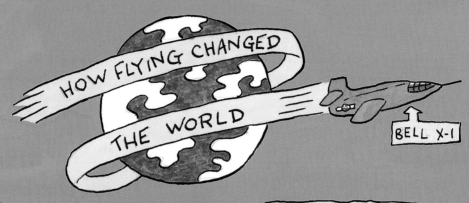

HOW FLYING CHANGED THE WORLD

BELL X-1

BOEING 247 (1933)

TRANSPORT

Everything can get from one place to another faster—like mail, and stuff you send away for, and people.

MILITARY

War planes are used for spying on the enemy, for dropping missiles, and for fighting other planes.

CURTISS P-40 WARHAWK

BELL 214

RESCUE AND RELIEF

Planes and helicopters can drop food and supplies in remote areas, and make emergency rescues.